ONE MAN'S TRASH

Tips from my 25 year journey
selling online to help pay the bills

This is NOT your "typical" selling guide. This is REAL information derived from my personal experience selling online over the past 25+ years

- What to sell & where to find it
- The Basics and More
- Tips and Tricks You May Not Have Thought of
- Links and Sources Included

- **<u>BONUS</u>** - Tips for selling on Poshmark, Facebook Marketplace, and Craigslist

PREFACE

I have over 25 years of experience selling on eBay. I've been selling on Mercari for about four years now. I do not work at this full time (I have a full-time job). I am not a "store". I am just a regular person selling items I have purchased and no longer need or items I find at thrift stores (like the Salvation Army, Goodwill) or yard sales. In 20+ years I have sold over $80,000 in items I don't want or need on eBay. In the past few years, I've sold as much as $10,000 - $12,000 some years. Some things were sold for a "profit"…i.e. more than I paid for them, many things were sold for a fraction of their original cost. But, my motto is "Anything I can get is better than nothing!"

Knowing how to sell on eBay (and now Mercari) has helped me during times of financial difficulty. I can determine how much or how little time I want or need to spend selling. For some years, I have sold almost nothing, because I didn't need the extra money and I was too busy. In other years, I have sold between $500- $800 a month most of the year. Selling is something I will be able to do once I retire to help meet expenses.

You can do it too!

The information in this book will likely be the most helpful to someone new to selling online, though I believe I've included some information and tips that will be helpful to all but the most seasoned sellers. I have tried to include everything I can think of to help you from start to finish. I've tried to organize the information logically, but there are a lot of things that cross over from one platform to another, so you may find information in one section of this book that will be valuable for another.

I believe the lessons I have learned during my 25+ years could be valuable to others. Many of the tips I am going to share with you came through the "school of hard knocks" aka "learning the hard way". I hope this very small investment of your time and money will save you some of the headaches I have experienced.

Please Note: *In the following pages, I share information regarding companies or products I have used. I do NOT endorse any of them and receive no financial benefit from any of them. Your experience may differ from mine and you should consider each one using your criteria. Additionally, I do NOT have an affiliate agreement with Amazon and I do NOT receive ANY benefit or compensation if you purchase something through a link I provide. My suggestions are provided as examples to assist you and possibly save you some "search" time.*

TABLE OF CONTENTS

WHAT TO SELL ONLINE

Toys, collectibles, vintage household, decor, collectibles, name brand clothes, and shoes.

Things that people tend to throw away can be very valuable. For example, recently an unopened package of individual cereals from the 70's sold for about $100!

Tip - **I NEVER sell iPhones online**...I recommend ONLY using local options such as Facebook Marketplace or Craigslist for these. There are WAY too many scammers online and this is a particularly easy and desirable item for those scammers. I have personally experienced an iPhone "scam" on eBay and while I ultimately got my money back from Paypal, the amount of time and energy dealing with the scammer was NOT worth it. **I have always successfully sold iPhones & iPads on Facebook Marketplace or Craigslist and would not sell these any other way.**

Bonus Tip - Do NOT take your old phones to a reseller such as ReTech. They will give you PENNIES on the dollar.)

On the other hand...I have successfully PURCHASED many iPhones, computers, etc. on eBay. So, if you find a seller with a good reputation, feel confident in buying. eBay loves its buyers. In eBay's view "the buyer is always right" and you can trust me when I tell you...if a buyer files a claim with eBay or Paypal, 99% of the time they will WIN their claim and, as a seller, there is almost nothing you can do to change that.

Tip - Always consider the cost of shipping and the "hassle" of packing, when buying something to resell online. For larger/heavier items, selling locally on Facebook Marketplace or Craigslist will usually yield better results.

Examples of things that sell you may not have thought of…

- Fisher Price Little People figures and sets (both vintage and modern)
- Webkinz plush and other items (clothes, figures, trading cards) both with and without codes can be popular
- Build-a-Bear Plush and accessories
- Large or unusual plush toys in excellent condition
- Lego sets
- Bratz and Hello Kitty items (all kinds…dolls, clothes, figures, keychains…you name it…)
- Vintage Barbie & My Scene Dolls and clothes (items that tend to get "lost" or "thrown away" can be a gold mine…doll earrings, necklaces, sunglasses, and other smaller accessories)
- American Girl Dolls, clothes, and accessories
- Disney Theme Park items - Mouse Ears, trading pins, collectibles, particularly things sold only in the parks, or sold online but discontinued.
- Themed items - "Star Wars" "Marvel" "My Little Pony" "Polly Pocket" "Littlest Pet Shop" "Nightmare Before Christmas" "Mickey Mouse"
- Handheld electronic games (from before the age of cell phone apps)
- Calico Critters/Sylvanian Families/Maple Town
- Miniatures for fairy gardens & dollhouses
- Vintage or discontinued holiday ornaments and decor
- Vintage painted paint-by-number "paintings" and other home decor items
- Designer handbags, wallets, shoes, and other accessories are usually easy money on eBay - Michael Kors, Tory Burch, Jack Rogers, Chacos sandals, and Lilly Pulitzer are some brands that have always been sure sellers for me.
- Vintage travel or destination souvenirs
- Vintage postcards and greeting cards and other paper memorabilia.

- Vintage pottery and dishes - particularly Corelle by Corning
- Vintage or high-end things that people tend to throw away. I have sold Laduree boxes and shopping bags, designer shoe boxes, and a variety of other things that many would have "tossed out". People buy Bath & Body Works empty three wick candle jars, and even cardboard toilet paper rolls. The old saying "one man's trash is another man's treasure" couldn't be more true when selling online.
- Women's Plus Size Clothes sell well online (clothes should be very gently worn, no holes, rips, stains, missing buttons, etc, or brand new with or without tags)
- 70's decor is very popular now, as is Mid-Century Modern, aka "Atomic" items

RESEARCH

Before buying or listing, research sold/completed listings for items similar to what you are selling. This is a very important step that will help you know which category and what details are most likely to help you sell your item(s).

Tip - USE YOUR PHONE!!! Before you buy something, do a quick search on eBay and/or Mercari to see if similar items are selling…use the "filter" at the top of the search page to find the "sold" items.

Where to find items to sell

Thrift stores, resale shops, and yard sales can be some of the best places for finding items to sell online. Spend some time searching sold auctions on eBay or items for sale and sold on Mercari with some keywords such as "collectible" "vintage" "rare" and "designer".

Look around your house - you may be surprised at the "value" of some of the stuff you have.

TIME TO MAKE SOME MONEY!!!

LISTING

Using the eBay and Mercari Apps on your phone for listings is the fastest way to list. You can "dictate" the auction description and use your phone to take the photos.

Search for a similar item and use the "sell now" or "sell yours" options, which will give you a bit of a head start on your listing.

If you can't find information about something on the online selling platform, try a Google Search. There is, for example, an American Girl "wiki" type page. You can find information about almost any American Girl doll, clothes, or accessories there. This can be very helpful, as the more details you include in your listing, the more likely you are to get the maximum sales price. There are also Disney pin trading boards that might give you insight into values. I'm sure other "specialty" groups could be helpful for many collectible items.

eBay gives sellers free listings every month. This will save you at least $.30 per listing.

Mercari does not charge ANY listing fees (at least at this time). You can list as much as you want for FREE. And, they occasionally have "promotions" that will reward your listing with a coupon for a dollar amount off a purchase. A nice bonus.

eBay - FIXED Listing Format - List using the FIXED format of 30 days (will auto-renew, every 30 days, until sold).

Mercari - All listings are "fixed price" but buyers can make offers that you can accept, counter or decline.

eBay - BEST OFFER - Always click the "best offer" option when listing - You can decline or counter offer if you don't like the offer sent by a potential buyer. When evaluating potential buyers, check feedback (number and quality).

PHOTOS

Good photos are important and lighting matters when taking photos!!

While you can do without it, a photo/lightbox can be an excellent way to ensure the best possible photos. I spent many years selling without any "special" lighting. But, a few years ago, I invested in a tabletop "photo lightbox". I found it on Amazon and paid about $100 for it. I feel it was a solid, worthwhile investment, as I didn't have to worry about shadows, colors not being accurate, etc. I use my phone for taking pics…I've had every kind of phone from an early version iPhone to the iPhone 13. Below is a link to the lightbox I bought:
https://www.amazon.com/gp/product/B01GIL6EU4/
ref=ppx_yo_dt_b_search_asin_title?ie=UTF8&th=1

Tip - Be SURE to include as many photos as needed to accurately represent the item(s) you sell. If there are ANY defects, be SURE to include photos and also include details in your item description.

This is a seller Best Practice!!

Always include information regarding whether the item is from a non-smoking home. You may also want to include information about whether you have pets if you know there may be pet hair on the item.

SHIPPING

Packing your items properly is key to being a successful seller.
Amazon can be a great source of supplies.

At a minimum, you will need to purchase packing tape and
probably bubble wrap.

You MUST purchase and use a postal scale. This is ESSENTIAL to
successfully determine shipping charges for items you sell. Your
postal scale does not need to be expensive. I prefer one that works on
batteries and I suggest one that weighs up to 50# (if you're thrift store
shopping...keep an eye out for one there...I found a second scale at the
Goodwill for $1.99)

Suggestion for postal scale
Accuteck 50 lb All-in-One Black Digital Shipping Postal Scale with
Adapter (W-8250-50B)

Tip - Buy the CHEAPEST clear packing tape with a decent
rating. Thick tape not only costs more, but I have found it is
frequently not as "sticky" as cheaper tape. You WILL want a
dispenser...particularly with cheap tape...because when that stuff
sticks to the roll, it's a pain to get re-started, eating up precious
time. I have found that I prefer the cheap plastic dispensers that
come free with tape, as opposed to the big heavy (more costly)
dispensers.

Suggestions for tape and bubble wrap -
Prices change frequently on Amazon, so I generally spend a few
minutes "shopping" before replenishing any of my packing supplies

<u>Shipping/Packing Tape</u>
https://www.amazon.com/BOMEI-PACK-18Rolls-
Packaging-Shipping/dp/B08Z3W7JSS/
ref=sr_1_187?dchild=1&keywords=packing+tape
+dispenser&qid=1625226243&s=office-products&sr=1-187

https://www.amazon.com/Packaging-Shipping-
Dispenser-BOMEI-PACK/dp/B07VG7X966/
ref=sr_1_27?dchild=1&keywords=packing+tape
+dispenser&qid=1625226315&s=office-products&sr=1-27

https://www.amazon.com/dp/B00D3P7GXI/
ref=sspa_dk_detail_7?
psc=1&pd_rd_i=B00D3P7GXI&pd_rd_wg=mor8j&pd_rd_r=AJ59
NSTRP9F5292TSJJB&pd_rd_w=CmrQ3

<u>Dispenser</u>
(I usually buy a package of tape that includes the dispenser, but
I wasn't able to locate a reasonably priced one on Amazon, at the
time of this writing -
https://www.amazon.com/gp/product/B00UUR3TLU/
ref=oh_aui_detailpage_o00_s01?ie=UTF8&psc=1)

<u>Bubble Wrap</u>
I usually buy a very big roll (175') 12" wide with small bubbles,
perforated every 12". I have found this to be the best way to
protect with the least amount of waste.
I have found the bubble of this size to be the best and most
versatile bubble wrap. I have not had much luck finding

reasonably priced large bubble wrap that is good quality. https://www.amazon.com/J-bubble-Small-Bubble-Cushioning-Perforated/dp/B0747XL57D/ref=pd_sim_229_23?_encoding=UTF8&pd_rd_i=B0747XL57D&pd_rd_r=TEVEAEQS8S6FPAE472Y5&pd_rd_w=YWtTM&pd_rd_wg=aSb7Y&psc=1&refRID=TEVEAEQS8S6FPAE472Y5#HLCXComparisonWidget_feature_div

If you have a Sam's Club membership, they sell the Scotch brand in this size for a pretty good price and the box is a dispenser, which is a nice plus.

USPS offers free Priority shipping boxes and will deliver them to your home. https://store.usps.com/store/results/free-shipping-supplies/shipping-supplies/_/N-alnx4jZ7d0v8v

USPS also offers free pick-up (with your regular postal delivery) which can be scheduled online. You only need to include one Priority package and can ship any other packages (ground, first class, media mail) when you request a pickup. https://tools.usps.com/schedule-pickup-steps.htm

Tip - Set up a USPS account. It is free and will make ordering supplies and pickups easier. You can also track pickups and other information there. https://reg.usps.com/entreg/RegistrationAction_input

Tip - Save all packing materials you receive from items you purchase...bubble wrap, tissue, air-filled pouches, bubble envelopes, and boxes (for items that do not require Priority shipping or do not fit in the free priority mail boxes). Recycle when you can. This not only saves you money but is good stewardship of our planet and resources.

Tip - ALWAYS ship with tracking!!! This is the ONLY way you are eligible for seller protection through eBay and/or Mercari.

Tip - I recommend full insurance for anything valued over $100, whether it is fragile or not, as insurance also protects you against a lost (or stolen) package.

I prefer USPS insurance over the eBay "ship protect", which is somewhat less expensive. I trust the USPS more than I trust the alternative.

Items shipped using Priority Mail are automatically insured for up to $100.

Tip - While eBay loves for shippers to use "Free Shipping", buyers don't seem to be savvy enough to realize the actual cost to a seller.

If you ship something heavy/fragile/breakable, I recommend including shipping in your auction price.

However, if the item is not breakable, separate shipping will generally result in higher profit for you, as the "psychology" seems to be that the auction price is less, making the cost less (even though that is not the case).

CROSS-POSTING/ CROSS-LISTING

Many times, I will cross-post/cross-list items.

Once you have created a listing (description, photos, determined price, and shipping) you will open your item(s) to a wider audience by cross-posting.

You will save time and energy, because you have already written a description and taken photos, so why not use all available options to maximize your profit!

Be sure to delete the other posts, when you've sold the item. This is particularly important with eBay, because you will be "dinged" if you cannot deliver an item someone has purchased. Poshmark doesn't like it, and you will get a snarky warning about "buyer disappointment", but, to my knowledge, you are not penalized if you can't ship an item. However, best practice for customer satisfaction on all platforms is to be sure to remove anything that is no longer available for sale.

EBAY

eBay can seem intimidating to a new seller. But, there are a lot of guides and a community forum that can be used to help answer the many questions a new seller may have.

Once you have set up an eBay account, you can begin creating listings. You can start listings and save a "Draft" for completing at a later time. WARNING…Drafts are not "permanent". eBay deletes them after a month or two, so don't delay completing your listing too long or all your hard work may disappear.

eBay - ENDING A LISTING:

Many sellers now "cross-list" on several selling platforms. I personally now sell many of my items on Mercari, as I prefer the quicker turnaround and "closing" of the transaction. If you do this, you will want to be sure to "end" your eBay listing. You can do that with no possibility of recourse on fixed price listings…but for auctions, eBay threatens to charge a final value fee.

Tip - Do not use the auction format for items you plan to cross-list.

eBay - RELISTING:

Once unsold auctions end, you can relist from the ended listing to avoid having to recreate the listing, while having the opportunity to re-evaluate your auction details including price. If you use fixed price listing, the only option is to list for 30 days and eBay will automatically renew the listing, at the end of each 30-day period until you either sell or end the listing.

Tip - Check your eBay seller page frequently for "promotional offers" from eBay for free listings, discounts off of seller fees, etc. ALWAYS use your "free listings", you will pay less in fees, that way.

What else you should know about eBay...

- **ALWAYS ship to the address on the eBay order.** If the buyer requests shipping to another address, they MUST add that address to their profile. They may need to contact eBay to get this accomplished. You will have NO shipping protection if you ship to any address other than the one on the eBay order.

- **Selling internationally**: I do not sell internationally. This is because the price of tracked shipping is generally very high and few buyers are willing to pay the higher cost. If you choose to ship without tracking, be prepared to lose the item and the cost of shipping, as the ONLY protection for sellers is when they ship with tracking! There are buyers who know and take advantage of this. I speak from experience.

- **Shipping time and delivery**: eBay will "ding" a seller who does not ship within the window required. You will also be "dinged" if an item does not arrive within the "estimated delivery window". This is not always fair, because you don't have control over a package once it has left your possession. However, as mentioned previously, eBay is "buyer-centric". So ALWAYS ship as soon as possible after the buyer has paid. My goal is to ship no later than the next shipping day, and the same day, if possible. This will ensure the package has the maximum time to reach its destination.

- **Feedback**: I recommend you wait until your buyer leaves feedback before leaving feedback for them. I believe that helps keep a buyer more "honest". Some sellers leave feedback immediately, but it is my opinion that the "transaction" is complete once the buyer has received the item and either contacted me if they believe there is an issue or has left me positive feedback if there are no issues. I leave feedback at the *end* of the transaction. If the buyer does not leave feedback for me, I do not leave feedback for them.

MERCARI

Mercari is a relatively new selling platform, but it seems to have taken off and I have had tremendous luck selling there. I will say that for higher dollar items, you may find that eBay, with its broader audience, is a better place to list those items...it will just depend on what you're selling.

Mercari is a good place to sell small odds and ends, brand-name makeup, and other miscellaneous items.

Why do I prefer Mercari?

1.	Ease of listing. eBay has become so bogged down with "item details" that sellers are REQUIRED to enter that listing there can be quite cumbersome. Mercari's App based platform is SUPER easy to use on your phone and you can list quite quickly that way.

2.	Shipping - No FEES. eBay charges a final value fee on shipping, whether you include it in the price or not. On Mercari, if the buyer pays shipping, you will not pay a fee on the shipping fee. So, more money in your pocket!

Shipping pricing. Sometimes, the shipping pricing is MUCH less on Mercari than on eBay...other times eBay wins in that department. I do like the ease of choices for shipping on Mercari, though. Mercari offers USPS, FedEx Ground, and UPS options, as well as "local delivery" (via Uber) which is relatively new. There is also an option to "ship on your own" which comes in handy in several different situations. For example, Mercari does not have a Media Mail option. So, if you are selling a heavy book, you can "ship on your own" and send it via Media mail. Or, if you're shipping something heavy but not large and you know it will fit in a flat rate bubble envelope or other flat rate box, you can "ship on your own" and use that method. (See the info regarding Pirate Ship at the end of the book.)

3.   Completion of Sale. eBay gives buyers WAY too long to file a "claim" against a seller THIRTY DAYS from the date of delivery. I have literally had someone receive an item and then, a month later, claim it didn't work and eBay required me to accept a return (and pay return shipping), only to find that the item worked just fine...buyer had "buyer's remorse" or something.

When you sell something on Mercari, the buyer has THREE DAYS from the date the item is delivered to leave feedback or submit a claim. That's it! If they don't leave feedback within 3 days, Mercari closes out the sale, leaves the seller 5-star feedback, and releases the funds. End of transaction! THIS IS HUGE FOR SELLERS and probably the main reason I prefer selling on Mercari over eBay.

4.   Less "competition". eBay has been around a VERY long time - over 25 years. They have a HUGE buyer base, but they also have a HUGE seller base. For most items, you will have a LOT of competition from other sellers. Because Mercari is relatively "new" (I think they've been around since about 2013, but seem to have really "taken off" over the past few years), they have a smaller buyer AND seller base. So, while there may not be as many buyers *looking*...there are also not as many sellers *selling*. This can prove to be money in your pocket if you're selling something rarely seen there.

What else you should know about Mercari...

- Their buyer/seller base seems to be a "younger" group than eBay. I have a 21-year-old daughter and she rarely looks at eBay for anything, but she will check Mercari.

- They do not seem to "automatically" side with a buyer, if

there is a "dispute", as eBay seems to do, these days. If you provide evidence to Mercari, they seem to actually review it and, while they may give the buyer a refund, you will not lose your sale. Sometimes they just take the loss and the buyer and seller are "unharmed".

- They don't "rate" a seller the same way eBay does. No "dings" for canceled transactions or "late" shipping. A seller's "star" rating is based on the buyer experience and nothing more. I like this a lot. Though I have occasionally run into a buyer who has NOT left a fair rating and Mercari will NOT change it, unless the buyer requests it. However, that has not happened often, so I would not consider it anything to be concerned about.

- You cannot see the rating a buyer leaves for you until after you leave their rating. So, if you have ANY concerns about the buyer or the transaction, you may want to keep that in mind, when you rate them.

- As soon as the buyer "purchases" your item, payment is made. Mercari holds the payment until after the buyer "rates" the transaction, which, as previously mentioned, MUST be within three days of delivery of the package.

- You MUST attach a bank account to Mercari. They don't accept Paypal. I have had absolutely no issues with getting my funds….ever. They give you a choice of leaving the funds in your Mercari account or transferring them to your bank account. There's an instant option, for which you pay a flat fee of $2, no matter how much you transfer, and there's a "free" option, that can take about 5 days. Personally, I always use the free option. I'm all about putting as much money in my pocket as I can.

POSHMARK

A little about Poshmark…

They do not charge a listing fee…which is good, especially for "cross-listing".

I don't like their fee structure, but I do like their "flat rate" shipping, and they can be great for the "right" items.

If you have some heavier bath products or shoes, handbags, or even household items, their buyer paid shipping fee of $7.49 is for up to 5 pounds via PRIORITY mail. This can be great if you are selling items that take advantage of it. You can use ANY box to ship with them…Priority, Flat Rate Priority, or any other packaging you have handy.

You will make more on higher-priced items. Beware though, when you get to $10 or below, their fees really hurt your "profit". I also feel like a lot of their buyers are "bargain hunting" and so I do a lot of "declining" of $5 offers I would "make" only $2, selling something for $5 on Poshmark…in contrast, I would make $4 selling something for $5 on Mercari…again…Mercari puts more money in my pocket!

With ANY online selling platform, be SURE to include as many photos as needed to accurately represent the item(s) you sell. If there are ANY defects, be SURE to include photos and also include details in your item description.

Always include information regarding whether the item is from

a non-smoking home. You may also want to include information about whether you have pets, if you know there may be pet hair on the item. ***This is a seller*** *Best Practice!*

What else you should know about Poshmark:

- Descriptions and photos are important. Like eBay, Poshmark is "buyer-centric", though they are not quite as automatically against the seller. However, I have had buyers claim something stamped leather was not leather and Poshmark gave them a refund and made me accept a return (I did NOT have to cover shipping). I also had someone claim the color of a pair of shoes was not as "described" and Poshmark gave them a refund. The buyer kept the shoes and Poshmark paid me for the sale. eBay has NEVER paid me for something that a buyer disputed. In this way, Poshmark and Mercari are both preferable to eBay.

- Poshmark buyers like "fancy" packaging. Use pretty wrapping and thank you cards, maybe even include a little "freebie"…this could be a costume necklace, bracelet, or pair of earrings in excellent pre-owned condition or a new pair of socks, scarf, etc that are not worth the trouble of listing… anything to ensure your Poshers (as they are called) are happy.

*S#*t Happens!!*
Things break during shipping

On eBay, when selling breakables, many times it is prudent to include shipping in the PRICE of the item and offer "free" shipping.

eBay holds the seller responsible for the safe arrival of items sold. YOU will bear any cost or loss for items received broken by buyers.

Insurance (up to $100) is included with ALL Priority shipments. Should an item arrive broken, you will be eligible to receive the full price of the item (and, because you included shipping in the price...you will not lose the price you paid for shipping)

EBAY - To file a USPS insurance claim:
https://reg.usps.com/login?app=OIC&appURL=https%3A%2F%2Fonlineclaims.usps.com%2FOICWeb%2F

- Request photos from the buyer of the broken item and the box and packaging. Ask them to hold all of these until you have received your insurance payment from the USPS because the USPS *may* request the broken item(s) and packaging be returned to a USPS office. (My experience has been that this rarely happens, but "better safe than sorry".)
- You will need the name and address of the buyer. The item description and "value" (price paid to eBay...if you did not include shipping in the price, you will NOT get the shipping

cost back).
- You should take a screenshot of the sold auction page to include when you file the claim.
- You will also include those buyer photos of the damaged item and packaging. The more information you provide to the USPS, the greater likelihood your claim will be approved.
- Generally, approved claims are paid by check and mailed to you within a couple of weeks.
- You may as well refund the buyer, in full (including shipping), immediately...as, if you don't do it, eBay will do it for you if the buyer files a claim.
  Claims are "bad" in the eyes of eBay and Paypal, so doing this on your own is the best policy.

Since most of the shipping you will do on Mercari and/or Poshmark will be through their services, you will follow their instructions for dealing with items damaged during shipping.

It is always best to ask for photos, as described above. Having all of the information you may need will result in the best possible outcome for you as a seller.

SELLING LOCALLY

Facebook Marketplace and/or Craigslist

For furniture, heavier/bulkier items, and cellphones (as previously discussed) I use Craigslist and/or Facebook Marketplace. I have used Craigslist a lot, in the past, but I find that many buyers prefer Facebook, so I have not sold on Craigslist for the past couple of years.

I have been successful selling everything from tools and home decor (Mirrors, tables, chairs) to clothes and other miscellaneous items. There's no listing fee, there's no selling fee, no need to package for shipping, so it's a great way to minimize effort and maximize the amount you can get for items you no longer want or need. **The best thing about selling locally is that when the buyer picks up the item and pays you, the deal is DONE! No worries about buyer's remorse, chargebacks, etc.**

I ALWAYS require pickup at my home. Facebook buyers can be "flaky". I only schedule a pickup time that I plan to be home, so I am not inconvenienced if they don't show up. I don't arrange to "meet" because I don't want to spend time driving only to find a no-show buyer.

There ARE scammers on Facebook Marketplace! If you get a message asking you to send a prospective buyer your phone number, do NOT send it to them. ONLY message them through Facebook. These are NOT legitimate buyers! They ask for your number, then say they want to be sure you are legit. They have a code sent to your phone then they can use that code to hack your email (and possibly other) accounts!!! Legitimate buyers are more than happy to exchange messages through Facebook. You should report anyone who asks for your cell number to Facebook as a "Scam" and block them.

Important Note: When selling personal items

that you no longer need or use, it's rare you will make a profit. It is likely you won't have receipts to prove the purchase price for

the IRS on your tax return. If you don't want to deal with getting a 1099 from Paypal, Venmo, or other cash app because of the new $600 rule, I recommend only accepting cash for these items. *If you are unaware of this new tax law, you can read about it here:* https://www.forbes.com/advisor/taxes/cash-apps-to-report-payments-of-600-or-more/

Selling unwanted clothes: This only applies to clothes that have been purchased and worn by my family. We didn't buy the clothes to resell them, so my attitude is that anything I can get for them is better than the "nothing" I will get by donating or throwing them away.

I have found the following "recipe" works well for maximizing $$ on gently worn or new clothes you no longer want or need:

- First, I take the clothes to my local consignment/thrift store (Plato's Closet is one. You may have other local consignment stores in your city.) These stores are usually very particular about condition/style, etc. But it's easy to walk out with $50-$100, depending on what you take in.

- Once I have sold the clothes I can sell to consignment/thrift stores, I count the items (5 pair of pants, 10 t-shirts, 15 tops, 5 Skirts, 10 Sweaters) and create a Facebook listing for everything. I don't take individual photos. I take pictures of the piles of folded clothes and post them along with the general sizes (i.e. Small-Medium or XL). I have successfully sold large amounts of clothes this way.

Again, this is just getting "something" instead of "nothing" for clothes you no longer wear.

If you have new items or designer items to sell, Poshmark or eBay, or even Mercari, are better platforms.

OTHER TIPS AND SHORTCUTS:

Keeping Track

It's important to keep track of your purchases for resale as well as expenses related to selling, including but not limited to shipping supplies (ink and paper for your printer, tape, bubble wrap, etc). The best way to do this is to set up a Google Spreadsheet for each year of selling with a tab for each type of expense (purchases to resell, shipping costs, office supplies, etc). Do whatever makes sense to you and will help you when it is time to file your income taxes. Both eBay and Mercari offer the ability to download sales reports, so you do not need to worry about keeping track of your sales, just expenses. Of course, you can do it all at tax time, but it can be difficult to recall everything you have spent over the previous year. If you use an online tax preparation app to complete your taxes, it will guide you through everything you need to consider and help ensure that you take advantage of all deductions available to you. I have used both TurboTax and TaxSlayer, in the past. H&R Block also has online tax preparation. Once you decide on a company, it's usually easiest to stay with them from year to year, as they will keep some of your information and import it into your subsequent year's tax return.

COPY/PASTE - DID YOU KNOW? If you have a Mac the copy/paste can be used to move text from your desktop to your phone and from your phone to your desktop? I just recently learned this and it has saved me ENORMOUS amounts of time, particularly for cross-listing! I'm not sure if it works on Windows machines, but give it a try.

Mac users will LOVE it!

Use HALF as much ink and paper! To save ink and paper when printing labels: Cut your letter-sized paper in half! Your printer will then print only the label part of the shipping label…you don't need the "informational" half, as you can find that online in the item details. This works for labels printed through eBay and Mercari. Poshmark labels are formatted differently, so those have to be printed on a full sheet of paper, but they don't include anything "informational" so you don't waste ink.

Make your own Thank You notes! Create some cute thank you notes about the size of a business card, spend as much or as little time on them as you like, then make copies, cut them up, and use them in your packages. You can also recycle holiday cards and other note cards. Again, be creative and think outside the box!

Source for new items to resell:
AliExpress.com can be a great place to buy new items for resale. It's super easy to use and make purchases. There is a "wholesale" version of Ali Express called Alibaba.com. Setup and purchase can be a little more challenging, but is a great place to get multiples for reselling.

FINAL TIPS

Shipping: & Packaging

I've said it before, but it bears repeating…Save all boxes, bubble envelopes, plastic/poly envelopes, and packaging from items you purchase online. Ask friends and family to do the same. I *never* have to buy boxes or plastic/poly envelopes. I do purchase bubble wrap from time to time, but less frequently because I recycle as much as possible.

Be CREATIVE with packaging…I use boxes from products I purchase for personal use, including plastic take-out containers or food containers to better protect small fragile items. These are lightweight, but provide a "structure" to protect items that can then be shipped in a plastic/poly envelope mailer.

Save tissue from gifts you receive, and recycle tissue from those you give (if the recipient is going to throw it away anyway). I use colorful tissue in gift bags for my family at Christmas and I NEVER throw it away…I save it to use as packing for online sales.

When I purchase tissue, I buy it at Dollar Tree. There is NO NEED to spend a lot of money on tissue!!! You can purchase online in bulk and either have it shipped or pick it up at your local store. Remember, every dollar you spend on packing materials is a dollar out of your PROFIT!!!

I buy ONLY white tissue for wrapping items! You don't want to risk colored tissue bleeding onto an item during shipping and costing you a successful transaction!

I also save all **cellophane and clear plastic bags** from items I purchase. I like to put every item in a water-resistant bag before I ship. I have received items from sellers that have gotten wet in transit. Again, you don't want to risk an unhappy buyer, so a little extra care in packaging goes a long way. If you don't have clear plastic bags from other sources, you can use large Ziplock-type storage bags. First, try using recycled bags, but if you have to purchase, buy the cheapest ones you can find.

Watch after Christmas sales and clearance bins for packing materials…sometimes you can find colorful bubble envelopes, packing tape, and tissue at greatly discounted prices.

Shipping Options:

I've previously discussed Priority Shipping and Media Mail through the USPS.
FedEx Ground and UPS are also options, though you will get the best rates and save the most time if you do NOT go to the "counter" and pay "retail". NEVER take an item to FedEx or UPS for packaging! The cost is prohibitive!

Pirate Ship is a great option for discounted USPS shipping when you need that option. I have used it many times and have been very pleased with the savings. https://www.pirateship.com

...ONE LAST THING...ETSY

Do you like to craft and make things? Have you ever wanted to sell the things you make online? Etsy is a great platform for that!!

You can sell your handmade items as well as craft supplies and vintage items on Etsy.

I have only made purchases there, so I can't share my experiences selling, but, I wanted to mention it, as it is another reputable platform and many sellers use it very successfully.

THANK YOU FOR READING MY SELLING GUIDE!!!

I hope you have found the information I've shared helpful. I wish you all the best for success in your journey learning to sell online. It is a great option for almost anyone. It doesn't take a lot of money to get started…a trip to your local Goodwill store, or even to your attic, may be all you need to do to begin.

Don't be intimidated!

Get started using the information In this Book and I believe you will find you are selling successfully in no time!

Happy Selling!!!